RESILIE

How Mental Health Tore through Our Marriage

Israel Ruiz

ISBN: 9798867926830

DEDICATION

To my amazing wife, Katie,

This one's for you! In the wild ride of life, you're my favorite co-pilot, my partner in life for the past 12 years. These pages are a shoutout to us—our laughs, our adventures, and the crazy, beautiful chaos we call family.

Your endless support, infinite patience, and love are the secret sauce that flavors not just our story but every word in this book. You're the reason these pages exist, a living reminder that life's tapestry is woven with our shared moments of joy, laughter, and a whole lot of love.

Through thick and thin, your love has been my rock, guiding me through the rollercoaster of life. This book is a small nod to the big impact you've had on me and our four boys.

Katie, you're my partner in life, my confidante, and the love of my life. With a whole bunch of love and a sprinkle of gratitude, this one's dedicated to you.

Always and forever,
Israel

CONTENTS

PREFACE

Have you ever thought about where to start telling your story? I certainly didn't. I hesitated to share it with even those close to me, let alone strangers, in a book. However, during a marriage conference with my wife, Katie, I received a strong prompting to tell our story. I showed her my rough notes and plans for the book, including the working title and topics for each chapter. Her response was honest: she wasn't ready to share her own story, which was still raw and true in our lives, after experiencing a mental health scare just six months earlier.

Although our life had improved, we were still trying to get everything back in order. When I said I was ready to share, she was honest that she wasn't. In 2018, during our first mental health crisis, I told Katie we would one day tell our story, but she responded with "Maybe"—a clear signal that we needed to focus on healing. Even now, in 2023, we're still healing and navigating life's ups and downs with four kids and a commitment to fulfilling the promises that God has given us in our marriage. This is our story of pain, healing, and a marriage that fought through sickness and health. Two people fighting for each other, for our family, for our faith, so that we could find peace in our healing journey.

As you read our story, you will see that it's not just about our struggles and how we overcame them. It's also about the lessons we learned, the faith we had to hold on to, and the people who came into our lives to help us along the way. We hope by sharing our story, you will find hope, inspiration, and encouragement for your own journey. Because the truth is, life can be tough, but we don't have to face it alone.

Our journey is a testament to the power of love, faith in Christ, and the strength of having friends and family. It's about finding light in the darkest moments and holding on to hope when all seems lost. Together, we'll explore the depths of human resilience and our boundless capacity for love, making each day a little brighter amid life's challenges. So come with us on this journey of pain, healing, and hope, and discover how even the most profound struggles can lead to beautiful transformations.

1. How We Met

You know those magical moments in movies when two people meet and the entire world seems to fade away? Well, that's precisely what happened the first time I laid eyes on Katie. It felt like the universe hit the pause button, and in that suspended moment, it was just the two of us. I couldn't tear my gaze away as her hair swayed in slow-motion perfection. In that instant, I knew she was extraordinary—someone I wanted to share a lifetime with. Katie might tease me for being overly romantic, and you may, too, but that feeling in my heart that day was undeniable. I was done searching for love because it had unexpectedly found me. All that remained was to turn our love story into reality. These words echoed the timeless sentiment of Victor Hugo: "Life is like a flower, and love is its sweet nectar." And believe me, my life was on the brink of a beautiful, blossoming journey.

Let me take you back to the beginning of a journey that would change everything. It was the year 2009, and I had just left behind a comfortable job in ministry in my hometown of Holland, Michigan. As a production and worship director, I had always been searching for God's plan for my life. And that's when a friend invited me to help plant a new church campus in Aurora, Illinois. It wasn't an easy decision, leaving behind everything I knew to start something new. But after much prayer and contemplation, I took a leap of faith and made the move. As the clock struck midnight on New Year's Eve, I found myself in a new town, surrounded by new friends, and with a new job. It was the beginning of an adventure that would lead me to the love of my life.

Taking this leap of faith was kinda like what C. S. Lewis once said: "You can't redo the past, but you can start fresh from where you are and shape your own future." And let me tell you, this fresh start was just the beginning of an incredible journey.

Fast forward to April of that same year, and I found myself at a church conference in sunny Orlando, Florida, surrounded by our superhero church plant team led by Obe and Jackie. It was a weeklong event packed with insights into cutting-edge church planting strategies, the latest tech trends, and wisdom from inspiring leaders and pastors, all showing us the path to becoming true disciples of Jesus.

As we navigated through various workshops and sessions, my friend Shannon—now my sister-in-law—came up to me with a mischievous grin and said, "Hey, guess what? My sister is swinging by for a family vacation after the conference. You two should totally meet." I didn't need a road map to understand her intentions: it was the classic setup. Here I was, single and ready to mingle, and so was she. I thought, "Why not? Let's roll with it!"

On the last night of our trip, a group of us decided to go out for dinner at the Samba Room, a trendy spot located in downtown Orlando (which, unfortunately, has since closed down). The memories of that evening are still so vivid in my mind—I can recall every detail. As soon as we arrived at the restaurant and were seated at our table, I turned to my friends Carter and Jenn and said, "Hey, Shannon's sister is coming. Make some room!" We all laughed with excitement because Carter and Jenn were the campus pastors where Katie regularly attended church, so they knew her and were eager to help make the evening unforgettable.

During dinner, I even spotted Hedo Türkoğlu, a well-known basketball player for the Orlando Magic at the time, eating there with his family and crew. But I didn't care about getting his autograph; my focus was solely on meeting Shannon's sister. In fact, I don't even recall asking for her name. I just knew that I was going to spend the rest of my life saying it. Cheesy? Maybe. But I was a guy ready to fall in love, and I couldn't wait for the moment that our paths would cross.

And then it happened, that moment I had been waiting for: the moment she walked into the room. I remember it so vividly, the way she moved with such grace and elegance. My heart skipped a beat, and I couldn't take my eyes off her.

Katie, on the other hand, has her own perspective of how it all started. She often tells me that it all began when she rededicated her life to God. It's fascinating to hear her side of the story and to think that if it weren't for that moment, we may have never met.

As soon as Katie was baptized, she felt a new sense of purpose in life. No longer would she be driven by her own needs and desires. She was determined to follow Jesus every step of the way. It wasn't just about seeking His guidance during tough times. It was about letting Him take control of her entire life. As that popular song goes, "Jesus, take the wheel." Katie wanted to surrender all to Him.

In her early twenties, Katie knew exactly what she wanted to do. She had a passion for helping children and students get to know Jesus. That's why she threw herself into volunteering at church, working with kids of all ages. But it was the little ones who stole her heart. Katie had a gift for connecting with them like no one else. She was known as the "baby whisperer" because of her magical touch. Just one smile from her could brighten the darkest of moods.

From a young age, Katie was surrounded by the joyful chaos of children. Her mom, Morna, was a childcare provider, and their home was always filled with little ones in need of love and care. Katie felt a deep connection to these children and knew in her heart that she was meant to care for children. It didn't matter if they were her own or not; she felt a sense of purpose in nurturing and guiding them.

As she grew older, Katie's desire to care for children only grew stronger. She began babysitting at a young age, and it quickly became clear that she had a gift for connecting with kids. Being a nanny was a natural next step for her, and she poured herself into the role, bringing light and love to the families she served.

But Katie knew that there was more to life than just caring for children. She wanted to help them in a deeper way, to guide them not just through their childhoods but through their spiritual journeys as well. That's why when the opportunity arose to work with children and students at her church, Katie jumped at the chance. She saw it as a way to use her gifts to help young people know more about Jesus and find the love and guidance that she herself had found.

Katie had always dreamed of finding a man who shared her faith and values, someone who would not only be her husband but a partner in raising a family that honored God. So when she heard about a guy from Michigan who was helping plant a church campus in her area, she was intrigued. Shannon, her sister, had mentioned that there was a guy who loved to sing and had a heart for the Lord. Katie said that she couldn't help but be curious about this "mysterious stranger." Despite being nervous, Katie felt ready to let God guide her all the way in this journey.

You know, it's pretty interesting—just a bit over half of single people say they make it a regular thing to attend church in their quests for something deeper, something that will give their lives more meaning. And here Katie and I found ourselves on a journey that was bound to take us far beyond the usual church services and gatherings. It felt a bit like a rocket propelling us into a world where faith and love merged in ways that exceeded our wildest expectations. I guess a lot of people in search of love yearn for that kind of connection, don't they?

So back to the story. When Katie arrived at the restaurant, she said her heart was racing with anticipation. She told me that she had heard so much about "this guy," and she couldn't help but wonder what he would think of her. Would he like her? Would they have anything in common? But when she scanned the room, her eyes fell on me. Our eyes met, and in that moment, she knew that there was something special going on. Little did she know, this was just the beginning of an incredible journey together.

As soon as I saw Katie, I knew she was special. I confidently walked over and introduced myself, eager to get to know her. She smiled, and I felt a spark of hope. Throughout the night, I couldn't help but steal glances at her, wanting to know more about this intriguing woman. When I finally asked her about her first impressions of me, I was a little nervous. But her answer surprised me: she thought I was too friendly! I couldn't help but chuckle at her honesty. Sure, I'm a people person, but that night, I only had eyes for her. I wanted her to like me more than anyone else at that table.

As we left the restaurant, the night was just getting started for Katie and me. We found ourselves sitting together, talking and laughing over drinks and enjoying each other's company. I couldn't help but notice how easy it was to talk to her and how her smile seemed to light up the room. As the night came to a close, I knew deep down that I wanted to spend more time with this woman. I could feel my heart skipping a beat at the thought of what the future could hold. But with past heartbreaks lingering in our minds, Katie and I were both hesitant. We talked about our fears and our doubts, but something inside of us kept telling us to take a chance. We both knew that God had brought us together for a reason and that we needed to trust in Him to guide us through whatever lay ahead.

In any relationship, there comes a point where you have to figure out if the person you're with is truly the right one for you. Katie and I were no exception to this. We spent weeks getting to know each other, sharing bits and pieces of our stories with one another. Every week, we grew closer and closer until one fateful dinner where we laid all our cards on the table. We talked about our dreams, our future, and what we hoped to accomplish in life. We were both tired of the same old dating scene and wanted something more meaningful. As the weeks turned into months, I knew that I had found someone special in Katie.

As my birthday approached, Katie was busy planning a surprise party for me. But little did she know, I had a surprise of my own planned. I wanted to make the day not just about me but about us. So I decided to turn my birthday party into something much more special. When the moment finally arrived, surrounded by our loved ones, I got down on one knee and asked Katie to be my wife. And with tears of joy in her eyes, she said yes. This wasn't the end of the story but rather the beginning of a beautiful journey. Together, we would learn and grow, face challenges and overcome them, and build a life filled with love, faith, and hope.

As our love story continued to unfold, we realized that finding our soulmate was only the beginning of our adventure. We both understood that maintaining a healthy, thriving relationship would require ongoing effort and intentional pursuit. We knew that even when we thought we knew everything about each other, there would always be more to discover along the way. We braced ourselves for the challenges that would come, knowing that the real test of our commitment would be in the hard times. We were aware that our past hurts could impact our future, but we were determined to work through them together. We knew that the journey ahead of us would be a wild and unpredictable ride, but we were ready to face it head on, hand in hand.

And as much as we'd all like to skip the painful parts of our stories, they're often the ones that shape us and push us to grow. Our story was no different. Just when we thought we had found the happily ever after we'd been searching for, life threw us a curveball. The pain we felt was hard, and it would have been all too easy to give up hope. But as we weathered the storm together, we began to see that our love was stronger than any hardship that could come our way. Through the tears, we found a deeper connection and a newfound appreciation for each other. The journey was far from easy, but it was in those dark moments that we truly began to understand what it means to love and be loved, cherishing every moment of our unique love story.

2. Our Firstborn

Katie and I tied the knot in June 2011, and not long after, life threw us a curveball. We found out we were going to be parents, and let me tell you, we were over the moon about it. We'd always talked about having a big family—six kids was our magic number, or so we thought. We even had plans to adopt later on because Katie had this incredible love for kids and I was just thrilled to become a dad.

Our first place together was a cozy loft with really high ceilings. When Christmas rolled around that year, we knew we needed a super tall tree to match. So we got this gigantic Christmas tree, decked it out with all the trimmings, and threw a fantastic winter party with our friends and family. Those days as a married couple were something special, and we couldn't wait to dive into parenthood.

Katie dived headfirst into parenting books, and we hit up all those first-time parent classes like eager beavers. We watched a bunch of baby-related movies, and man, those were the times. Our winter was chock full of firsts. After the holiday buzz faded, we geared up for the new year, ready to take on the adventure of being parents. Our evenings were spent watching classic fall flicks, sharing stories, and indulging in treats, all while counting down the days until Baby Ruiz would join us.

A couple of days before the new year, we were just having a quiet evening at home, you know, one of those moments when life seems peaceful. And then it hit us like a bolt of lightning—Katie screamed, and it sent chills down my spine. She was bleeding, a lot, and we both just broke down in tears because we knew something terrible had happened.

We sat there on the couch, tears streaming down our faces, and the word *devastated* doesn't even begin to cover what we felt. This was a situation neither of us could fix, and no words would make it better. All we could do was pray and wonder why this was happening. I felt this surge of anger and confusion, lost in a sea of emotions.

Katie, in her cries to God, started blaming herself, as if something in her past had triggered this tragedy. It's funny how we tend to either blame others or ourselves when things go bad. In my mind, I felt like I'd come up short somehow. I said all the right things, trying my best to comfort my wife and seeking some sort of guidance from God as we grappled with the unanswerable why that had suddenly become the focal point of our lives.

The pain of having a miscarriage, of losing our first child, still cuts deep even as I pour it onto these pages. Revisiting that moment was tough, and I can't help but imagine Katie flipping through this chapter. We both know the weight of those feelings. Sure, it's true that going through something like that can make you stronger in the long run, but honestly, I couldn't care less about the clichés we're supposed to say when tragedy hits.

We just needed to be sad, angry, and well, just let us be, you know? In my limited time on this earth, I've realized that these painful moments, they come and go. But if we dodge the grief, if we avoid facing it head on, we're not really preparing ourselves for the curveballs life throws our way. Grieving, it's a messy part of life, but a lot of us can't stand it, so we rush through it and never really deal with the issues. And then, when the next tragedy strikes, we're not as ready as we should be for whatever the world decides to throw at us.

That day, in our moment of grief, we shed some tears and hoped the pain would just vanish. But no such luck. Still, we kept on going.

Over the next few months, life didn't hit the brakes. As the new year rolled in, the church campus I'd been a part of from the start cut my hours in half. So I had to hustle, juggling not one, not two, but three part-time gigs. Katie was busy, too, growing her day care business. It was a crazy, fast-paced time.

But amid the chaos, we managed to make new friends and find a new church that felt like home. And guess what? We even took the plunge into homeownership by snagging our very first house, thanks to our friends Rick and Desiree. We were living life in the fast lane, trying to move forward while still clinging on to those precious memories.

Over the next year, we poured our energy into fixing up our new old house. It was something we could actually work on and improve, a distraction from the past. Time ticked on, and Katie and I started thinking about becoming parents once again. We prayed a lot and approached it cautiously. And then, that little stick confirmed it—we were going to have a baby. Excitement washed over us all over again. Katie started setting up the nursery and buying baby stuff, and our days were all about preparing for this new chapter. We couldn't help but feel grateful for the incredible opportunity.

Let's focus in on the early days of fall 2013. Katie and I were eagerly preparing for the changing season, both at home and in our lives. I had just secured a full-time position at a new church, a significant step in our journey. However, it came with a catch: the church wouldn't provide insurance just yet, so we had to arrange our own coverage, which, to be honest, wasn't exactly budget friendly.

But here's the exciting part. Baby Ruiz was due to make their grand entrance into the world come spring, and we were absolutely thrilled. We wanted everything to be perfect for our little one. We grabbed wall art for the nursery. We set up baby monitors and collected all the essential baby gear—bottles, burp rags, you name it. We had things all neatly arranged, ready for action. At that moment, we were brimming with confidence, feeling as prepared as any expectant parents could be.

But then, on a regular afternoon, Katie came up to me and said, "I'm bleeding."

I swear my heart stopped for a beat, and I blurted out, "What do you mean? What's going on?"

She just repeated it. "I'm bleeding."

In my head, I was screaming, "Not again." I couldn't fathom what Katie must've been going through at that moment, but one thing was clear—this was not good news. After the initial shock wore off, we got on the phone with Katie's mom, who calmly told us to head to the hospital.

We made that somber drive to the hospital in silence, both of us knowing all too well that history was repeating itself, mirroring what had happened about a year ago. The trip, which usually took less than ten minutes, felt like an eternity. Once we were settled in the hospital room, we sat there in quietude, gripping each other's hands tightly, bracing ourselves for what the doctor would tell us.

I remember sitting there, offering up a prayer with Katie, my mind filled with fear and frustration, a scream building up inside me. But I had to stay strong for Katie. As the doctor started talking, I sort of blocked out her words because I already knew what she was going to say. I just held on to Katie's hand, knowing that's what she needed most at that moment. Then, amid the doctor's explanation, I heard something that stopped me in my tracks: "The baby is doing fine."

I couldn't help but interrupt, asking, "What?"

She went on to explain in more detail that our baby was safe and sound and we were good to head back home.

We couldn't contain our joy as tears of happiness rolled down our cheeks, and we let out these ecstatic, almost gleeful screams right there in the hospital room. It was an incredible relief, like a weight lifting off our shoulders. On the drive back home, we just held each other, basking in the knowledge that our dreams for the future were still alive and kicking.

We prayed together, expressing our gratitude to God for watching over us. Baby Ruiz still had a few weeks to go before arriving, but in that moment, we felt this overwhelming sense of peace. We knew that no matter what, God was looking out for us, whether we were crying out in pain or shouting with joy. It was a reminder that even when our faith wavered, He had everything under control.

Katie was a real trooper during the rest of her pregnancy, dealing with all the typical pregnancy stuff like back pain and fatigue like a champ. When it was time for the baby to arrive, she turned down the offer of a wheelchair and practically strutted into the maternity wing of the hospital. Even as contractions were doing their thing, she powered through them like they were no big deal. The nurse tried to get her to take a load off, but Katie was like "Nah, I'm good."

After a few hours of contractions, the doctor came in and dropped the bombshell that it was C-section time for safety reasons. Katie was pretty bummed about it because, you know, she's a strong woman and wanted to do it the natural way. But we trusted the doctor.

Within the next hour, Kobe Israel made his grand entrance, tipping the scales at a healthy ten pounds and six ounces. This big boy brought an avalanche of joy to both of us.

We were thrilled to meet Kobe, but the doctors had some worries about his health. So they whisked him off to the NICU, the neonatal intensive care unit. It was a bit shocking and sad because Katie had just gone through a C-section. Let me tell you, that procedure isn't a walk in the park. And now Kobe had been whisked away to the NICU.

Katie, though, she's one tough cookie. Despite the pain, she was dead set on being there for our little guy. So the nurse wheeled her into the NICU, and finally, she got to cuddle with Kobe for hours on end. It was the start of their special bonding time, a mother's love shining through in those precious moments.

For the next three days, those two—Kobe and Katie—became an inseparable duo. But as Katie's stay in the hospital neared its end, the medical team expressed concerns about Kobe's condition. His breathing was causing worry and a touch of jaundice had crept in, so they recommended he remain in the NICU for further observation and treatment. It was a curveball we hadn't seen coming. We had hoped to bring him home with us when we left the hospital. Let me tell you, the weight of sadness to be without him was almost unbearable.

While Katie was holding on to Kobe one afternoon, she, understandably, was not feeling her best. I mean, how could she? She had just undergone surgery, and her precious child was still in the NICU. Our prayers were more fervent than ever before. The heaviness of the situation weighed on us, but we clung to our faith, seeking peace in those moments of our prayers.

Katie, already not feeling great, suddenly got hit with a fever and started shaking like crazy. We didn't waste a moment; we knew we had to act fast. After a bunch of tests, we got the news that Katie had a UTI, a urinary tract infection, and she needed treatment and observation. That meant another night in the hospital, and all we wanted to do was hold our little guy. But because Katie had an infection and Kobe was still in the NICU, the hospital rules said we couldn't see him for safety reasons. It was tough to be kept apart, let me tell you.

The punch to the gut we experienced lingered for a whole day. There was a rule that Katie had to be fever-free for a solid twenty-four hours before she could enter the NICU and be with our little Kobe. I have to say, the mental and emotional toll on Katie during this time was just off the charts. We had put our hearts and souls into preparing for this moment, but here we were, four days after our baby was born, and Katie had to wait to see him again.

Now, even though I had the option to go and be with Kobe, I decided not to for that twenty-four-hour stretch. I didn't want to leave Katie hanging, and the last thing I wanted was for her to feel even worse because I got to see our baby boy while she couldn't. So I stuck by her side, and we spent that time together, praying, chatting, and mostly just waiting for those twenty-four hours to finally tick away.

Finally, the moment we'd been waiting for came. We strolled down that hospital corridor, pushed open those big doors, and there he was, little Kobe, cradled in our arms. It was like the whole world just faded away. All the usual noise and distractions went quiet, and in that moment, it was all about Kobe, Mom, and Dad. Through all the ups and downs, our faith had been our rock. We leaned on Jesus daily, grateful for the incredible joy we found, even on those tough days when doubt and frustration tried to sneak in. In a world that can be pretty crazy, having Kobe with us was like a ray of sunshine.

We wished for a perfect life, where everything we had and everything we wanted was just right. But let's not forget, life isn't always that simple. And before we move forward, let's take a minute to remember that even in an imperfect world, joy comes in the morning.

3. Here's Number Two!

It was just the three of us, navigating the world of firsts together. Family and friends were in and out, lending a hand, feeding us, and giving us some much-needed downtime. Being parents was incredible, but let's be real: it was also pretty darn exhausting. I was grinding away at life, juggling my pastoral duties and learning the ropes of fatherhood all while striving to be a good husband. It wasn't a cakewalk, that's for sure.

Looking back, I can't help but chuckle at how I used to wish for an easier life back then. If I could chat with my younger self, I'd say, "Hey, enjoy this moment because, trust me, it's only going to get harder."

As we rolled into 2015, Katie got the baby fever again, and we decided it was time to grow our family with a second child. Having been through it once, we felt pretty confident about the whole parenting thing. So when we got the news that baby number two was on the way, we did what we knew best. We spruced up the nursery with some cute wall art, added more baby monitors, and unboxed all the baby essentials—bottles, burp rags, you name it. Everything was neatly in its place, just like before. But this time around, we couldn't help but think about the unexpected, given our past experience.

As the due date approached, Katie was in great shape according to the doctors. We embraced the fall season as a family, enjoying things like watching football, picking apples, rocking Halloween parties, savoring family Thanksgiving feasts, and all the good stuff. We were gearing up for the arrival of baby number two with a mix of excitement and readiness. Parenthood had taught us a lot, and we were about to start on this new chapter with a sense of confidence, even as the memories of our previous challenges lingered in the background.

Since Kobe had entered the world through a C-section less than two years ago, we had to go down the same route again for baby number two. It wasn't our first choice, but it was the plan. The good part was that we got to pick the date and time, which made things a lot less stressful. As Katie put it, she wouldn't have to deal with contractions or other labor pains this time around. It was a pretty straightforward process—show up at the hospital and wait our turn, almost like waiting for a table at a restaurant.

Watching Katie get whisked away to the operating room, joining her there, and finally, seeing our second baby make his entrance, it was all over in less than an hour. It felt quite different from our first childbirth experience. I remember Katie, who'd been given some medication for the surgery, looking at me kind of spaced out but still present. She kept asking if everything was OK because she couldn't hear the baby. I had to keep reminding her that he was still inside her and that I'd let her know when he made his grand entrance. I held her hand, offering support and reassurance that everything was going smoothly.

Let's take a breather and pause here because I need to explain something important. If you've ever had a C-section or been in the room for one, you know it's a bit of an odd experience. On one side, you're all excited about your baby arriving, but on the flip side, you're going through surgery, which, whether you think of it as major or not, is happening. Your body is being opened up, and doctors are doing their thing. Katie's told me she doesn't remember much of the surgical part. It's not like it's a highlight of giving birth. She says she was in kind of a daze, like she was in a fog. She had a faint sense of what was happening but couldn't recall the nitty-gritty details or much of the conversation.

As they prepared to bring our new baby into the world, I couldn't help but think about the journey ahead of us. We'd been through so much already, from the challenges of our first child's early arrival to the mental health struggles that had shaped our lives. But here we were, about to welcome another precious soul into our family, ready to embrace whatever came our way. The joy and anticipation mixed with the memories of our past trials, creating a complex tapestry of emotions as we awaited the arrival of our second child.

As for me, meeting our new baby was an absolute joy. Seeing him all wrapped up in blankets and holding him—it was magical. But for Katie, it was a different story. She had to lie there while they put her back together. She couldn't get that immediate, heartwarming first look because of the medication and her position, which didn't allow her to hold him properly or even see him clearly. So despite having gone through this procedure once before, it felt unique. What we weren't prepared for was this strange sense of emotional disconnect that caught us both off guard.

I distinctly remember how Katie looked at our new baby. It's not that she didn't care; it's just that she was in the middle of surgery. The whole setup didn't really allow for an instant emotional connection with him. Under the influence of medication, there was this sort of detachment, a momentary sense of being somewhere else. She was there, but it was like her consciousness took a brief vacation, and I saw just a shell of her for a little while.

All right, let's hit that play button again. Picture me clutching Katie's hand as the wails of our new little man filled the room. Kai Anthony, weighing in at seven pounds and twelve ounces, had made his grand entrance. He looked just perfect, with his scrunched-up face and those oh-so-cute pouty lips. His cries didn't last long, and soon, Katie was ready to hold him and start feeding.

It was crazy how quickly it all happened—only about thirty minutes separated his birth from Katie coming out of surgery and holding him in her arms. By then, the effects of the medication had worn off, and Katie was back to her usual bright-eyed, energetic self. She was on a mission to get that baby latched on for his first meal. Remembering the challenges we faced with our first child, especially since Kobe spent his first ten days in the NICU and we had to endure a twenty-four-hour separation from him, Katie wasted no time this time around. I've got to say, Katie is a true rock star!

The overwhelming emotions of holding our new baby washed over us. It was a stark contrast to our first childbirth experience, which was filled with anxiety and uncertainty due to Kobe's circumstances. This time, there was an air of confidence and a deep sense of gratitude. We marveled at the miracle of life, cherishing every moment as we welcomed Kai into our family with open hearts and open arms.

You know, over the years of being with Katie, I've learned that when she sets her sights on something, she's determined to make it happen. I've always admired that about her. As she worked tirelessly to be the best mom ever, she took it to a whole new level. After a few hours of precious bonding time between our new baby and his mom, the moment finally came for Kobe to meet his little brother. It was simply perfect! And to this day, those two share a bond that's absolutely unbreakable.

After two days in the hospital, the doctors gave us the green light to head home. Let me tell you, Katie was one determined lady. Even after her surgery, she was dead set on getting up and taking Kai home. Nothing was going to stop us from experiencing that joy together—bringing our newborn home as a family. Our ride back was perfect, with all four of us in the car, and we spent the first afternoon at home napping together. It was one of those moments when both Katie and I felt an overwhelming sense of peace. At that time, we took a deep breath and thanked God for this precious gift of family.

As the days rolled on, our family of four was in full swing—two kids under two, a bustling household, returning to work, and juggling all the facets of life. Katie, in particular, was balancing the demands of a newborn and an almost two-year-old. The Christmas season came and went, we did some traveling, and we rode the roller coaster of daily life with all its ups and downs. I've got to say, when you find a quiet moment in your life, grab hold of it because life has a way of never slowing down. But these precious moments, they're the ones that make it all worth it.

Things felt pretty hectic right up until May of the following year. It was around that time that we started to notice a change. Amid the busyness and exhaustion, Katie and I began to detect a shift in our mental and emotional well-being. We'd often ask each other how we were doing, and the reflexive response was always "Fine." But deep down, we knew we were just telling ourselves a comforting lie. We were far from fine; we were merely getting by. It reached a point where Katie suggested that we seek help from a counselor.

At that time, I couldn't help but wonder, Why? I thought we were doing just fine—or so I believed. But when Katie suggested counseling, it became apparent that we might not be as fine as I'd thought. So we both sat down with a counselor, hashing out how often we should meet and what needed to be discussed. It was during this process that Katie saw an opportunity to make things better for our family. She realized that her well-being was crucial for the family's overall happiness. Katie, being the kind of person who tends to overthink things, had found herself grappling with increasing anxiety over time. This anxiety had a way of taking over her thoughts, preventing her mind from ever finding a moment's rest. While I'm certainly no expert, this is what I observed in Katie and learned from our conversations. It all started becoming evident after the arrival of our second child, with signs of postpartum depression creeping in. Katie sensed something was off and took the brave step of seeking help.

It began with a simple admission: "I don't feel like myself today." Those words made her pause, not by choice but because something inside her didn't feel quite right. Over the past five years, our lives had been a roller coaster. We faced financial woes and health challenges, celebrated new additions to our family, shouldered emotional baggage, and grappled with mental exhaustion—it was a lot to handle. Many might say, "That's just life," but it really shouldn't be. We often chase happiness through material possessions, things that won't stand the test of time. In the process, we tend to neglect our own well-being—our mental, emotional, and physical health—all for fleeting pleasures. Sadly, it's a trap many of us find ourselves in. Katie recognized there was a problem, but addressing it would prove to be a long and arduous journey. Yet it was a journey we needed to embark on together for the sake of our family.

4. Three Times the Charm

In less than five years, Katie and I went from being total strangers to tying the knot and becoming proud parents of two amazing boys. Life was throwing us curveballs left and right. I had been grinding away at a church for three years, while Katie was adjusting to her new role as a stay-at-home mom. We were trying to figure out what the next chapter looked like for our family of four.

When Kobe hit the one-year mark, we kicked off a cool tradition. As spring rolled around, we hit up an indoor water park as a family—a much-needed break from our usual hustle and bustle. It was our way of shaking off reality and just having some good-fashioned fun together. We were lucky to be active in our community, whether it was dishing out meals to those in need or lending a hand with neighborhood projects. Sometimes the kids pitched in, and sometimes it was just Katie and me finding ways to help out whenever there was a call for it.

We kind of got comfortable with the whole busy routine, not just in our community but also in our church life. There was always something happening, to the point where sometimes it felt more like an obligation than a choice. Our lives were buzzing with activity, and we had formed a bunch of connections, but beneath it all, something was off.

In 2016, Katie and I were like tornadoes, spinning through kid stuff, church stuff, family gatherings, and making new friends. Amid the craziness of parenting and being a couple, Katie somehow managed to sneak in regular date nights. And boy, do we owe a huge shout-out to Katie's mom, who was always there to swoop in and take care of the kids, giving us some much-needed downtime. Having that crew of supporters, including our friends and families, was an absolute game changer.

Our church was like a hub for forming awesome friendships with people we could always lean on and trust. But in terms of being our rock, it was definitely our families—both mine and Katie's. They stepped up and helped us out in countless ways. Looking back, I can't help but think, "How on earth would we have handled what was coming without them?"

In 2017, we got the big news that baby number three was on the way. It was exciting but also came with some challenges because we were living in a pretty small home. Still, we were up for the challenge. Katie and I always planned on having a big family, so this was part of the grand plan. We started getting everything ready, making sure we had all the baby gear and setting up the nursery. We even transitioned Kai out of the nursery so that the new baby could have the space. Making a nearly two-year-old share a room with his toddler brother was quite the adventure, but Katie, being the child whisperer she was, managed it beautifully. I pretty much just followed her lead and supported her decisions. Katie had this magical ability to calm down even the fussiest of babies. That's why she was called the baby whisperer to everyone who knew her. Getting two kids under four to sleep in the same room almost every night was like witnessing a miracle.

As we rolled into 2018, it was time for our third child to make an entrance. Another scheduled C-section was on the horizon, and this time, Katie was a pro. The doctors even noticed how well-prepared she was, commenting, "You've definitely done this before."

The procedure started, and I felt a sense of calm. I could see that distant look in Katie's eyes as the medication kicked in. When I asked how she was feeling, she admitted, "Not good," explaining that the meds made her feel a bit off. We talked to the anesthesiologist, who helped manage her discomfort and medication. He kept a close eye on her, but she powered through the confusion as we eagerly awaited our new baby's arrival.

Finally, the little champ made his entrance—Kreed Kenneth, tipping the scales at a whopping nine pounds and three ounces. This dude had more of that newborn gunk on him than any of our previous kiddos. It looked all pasty and white, and the nurses were on cleanup duty while I played "cut the cord" like I did before. They bundled him up nice and cozy, then handed him over to Katie.

Katie got to hold him for a bit, but something seemed off. She had this distant look and a half smile that just didn't sit right. We knew she was on some meds, but this was different. The doctors reassured us everything was A-OK, and they asked me to take Kreed out while they finished up with Katie. So off I went with Kreed, and we had ourselves a little chat. The nurse mentioned some tests because of his wonky levels and breathing that needed checking.

Before long, Katie joined us, and she seemed back to her usual self. I asked how she was holding up, and she admitted this time was rough. She said it felt like she was in some kind of alternate universe, barely in touch with reality. I agreed, telling her how it looked like she was physically there but mentally elsewhere during the surgery. She nodded in agreement. We talked it over with the doc, who said she was physically good to go but recommended some chats with the medical team and therapists.

But there we were, the trio—Mom, Dad, and baby Kreed. As Katie held him close, we exchanged smiles and said our thank-yous to our Heavenly Father. Kreed was downright perfect. In that moment of calm, we let out a sigh of relief. The nurses told us they wanted to check on Kreed's breathing in the NICU, just to be safe. They assured us it wasn't a big deal, but they wanted to keep an eye on him. So I decided to tag along with Kreed to the NICU, while Katie's mom stayed with her during her post-op recovery.

Now, if you've ever set foot in a NICU, you'd know it's this room with soft lighting, divided by curtains for some privacy. Only two folks could be with the baby at a time. There was a rocking chair and a crib for the little one. And there I sat, keeping Kreed company, thinking back to when Kobe was in this same spot not so long ago. I did the dad thing—said some prayers, told some stories, and made sure he knew just how amazing his mom was. Before we knew it, Katie joined us, and there we were again: one big, happy family, counting the days until we could take our little dude home.

A few days later, we finally got to bust out of the hospital room together. Kreed, the newest addition to our squad, was all giggles and good health, while Mom and Dad were itching to get back home. When we strolled through the front door, you could see the excitement radiating from his big brothers. Our place became a revolving door of family and friends over the next five days, all eager to shower us with support. Little did we know, we'd need that support sooner than we thought.

Back to our usual chaotic routine—now with three kids under the age of five. My work was still relentless, especially with Easter events ramping up at the church. Katie was on a mission to restart her day care services after a short break following Kreed's birth. So we dived back into our crazy schedules, and Katie, in particular, was bearing the brunt of exhaustion and overwork. Bills were piling up, and life showed no signs of slowing down.

As summer crept closer, Katie and I sat down to hash out our plans for the rest of the year—holiday schedules, school logistics, work commitments, birthdays, and all the other details of our bustling lives. But on one particular evening, things took an unexpected turn. Katie seemed a bit off, distant, like her mind was somewhere else entirely. Her words came and went in our conversation, almost like she was drifting in and out of consciousness. At first, I figured she was just tired, but then I noticed her hands—clasped together, rubbing nervously. I asked if she was all right, but she didn't respond. Worried, I reached out to Katie's mom, who rushed over to help me tuck her into bed. We figured maybe the medication for postpartum depression was taking a toll, but something didn't feel quite right.

After we put the kids to bed and said our goodbyes to Katie's mom, I climbed into bed next to Katie. She was awake but seemed lost in thought. I snuggled up to her, and we said a heartfelt prayer together. The next morning, she got up early, fed Kreed, and then returned to bed. I thought maybe she was just tired, so I went about getting the kids ready for the day. But when I checked on Katie, she was still in bed, not saying a word. Her eyes looked vacant, and I was trying to figure out what was going on because all I wanted to do was help.

I called Katie's counselor, hoping for some guidance. Just as I started talking to the counselor on speakerphone, Katie suddenly burst into tears. It was the first emotion I had seen from her in the last twelve hours. I asked her questions, but she didn't respond. We tried everything to get through to her, but there was no reply. Then, out of nowhere, Katie collapsed to the floor, crying as if she were in intense pain. I had no choice but to call 911 and ask for an ambulance to help her.

Katie's sister came over to pick up the kids, shielding them from the troubling scene. They had no idea what was happening. Shannon stayed with Katie for a bit, hoping to break through whatever was going on. Still, there was no response. As the kids left with Shannon, the ambulance arrived to take Katie to the hospital.

The doctor told me that Katie had this crazy anxiety attack that basically knocked her out, both mentally and physically. She was so overwhelmed that she started seeing stuff that wasn't there. They tried giving her some different meds, but they didn't do squat. So they said she needed to go to the ICU, and we spent the next twenty-four hours there, hoping things would get better. But man, it was like a real life horror flick.

Katie couldn't recognize anyone, and she seemed lost in her own world. It was tough to watch. She told me weeks later that it felt like she was drowning in her own thoughts, struggling to say things and forgetting how to talk. It was like she was trapped, unable to break free.

The doctor eventually said she needed to be in a mental health facility for a while, just so they could keep an eye on her and help her get better. It was right next door, but we had to go through this underground tunnel to get there. When we walked in, I was super nervous. There were other folks there, each dealing with their own stuff, and here I was, leaving my wife in a place where she didn't know anyone, hoping she'd come back home soon.

In my darkest moments, I found myself on my knees, having a heart-to-heart with God, as if my life hung in the balance. My prayers shifted from polite requests to downright urgent pleas. I was engulfed by a whirlwind of anger and despair because the woman I held dearest, the mother of my little children, my best friend, was lying there, seemingly without hope, and it was like my hands were tied.

As I sat beside Katie in that place, one thought kept nagging at me: This just couldn't be the end of our story, could it? Would she be stuck like this forever? It had been a couple of days, and I couldn't see any improvement. I had all these questions about what the doctors were doing or maybe not doing. So I turned back to God, praying for help yet again. I poured my heart out for Katie, convinced that deep down, wherever she was inside, she was praying right alongside me. Katie had reached a point where she could talk, but her words were all jumbled up, like puzzle pieces that didn't quite fit. It was all just surreal.

For the next two days, it was like déjà vu. I'd swing by to see Katie, and her family would drop in, too, but it felt like we were stuck in some kind of loop. Four days had come and gone since Katie's emotional avalanche, and when I got back home to our little munchkins each evening, I grappled with the idea of navigating life without her. Our world was already a roller coaster, and doing it solo just didn't add up. To an outsider, I probably seem like the calm, collected type. I don't wear my heart on my sleeve, but every now and then, my frustration or anger might sneak through. For the most part, though, I keep my thoughts and feelings locked away. In this situation, I felt this immense duty to be the unshakable rock for my kids. They were too young to get what was happening. Kobe, our four-year-old, would innocently ask about Mama. But after the kids had drifted into dreamland, I'd take a moment to let it all out, only to gather myself again and face the challenges of a new day.

It was a crazy week, but on the fifth night of all this chaos, I got a call from the doctors. Usually, it was just updates on Katie's condition and what they were doing to help her. Sometimes, Katie would be on the call, but she couldn't say much—just simple stuff like "Hello" or "I'm OK." But this night was different. It wasn't the doctor's voice I heard first. It was Katie's. She said, "Hey, hun."

I couldn't help it; I started crying. I knew right then and there that my Katie was back. My wife had come back to me. We had the best conversation we'd had in days. She wasn't completely herself yet, but she was miles better than before. In that moment, we both felt like thanking Jesus. We prayed together, and before we hung up, I told her, "Katie, your story is going to be a lifeline for someone out there. Get ready because God's going to use you."

The rest of the year was all about taking it easy. Katie took a few months to focus on herself and have a bit of fun. She met with doctors, counselors, and therapists, all helping her find her way back to self-care. They made sure she knew this wasn't a onetime fix; mental health needed daily care.

During those days of healing, we rediscovered just how deeply we loved each other, our unbreakable bond. We used that time to slow down, take care of ourselves, and be better for our family. Life might have slowed down for us, but the world kept spinning, leaving us wondering what was waiting for us next and if we could handle whatever came our way.

5. The Quad Squad

In 2018, life hit us like a freight train, both physically and emotionally. It felt as if we'd been thrown into a boxing ring, taking hits left and right and a few knockout punches for good measure. Looking back on it now, I'm honestly baffled by how we managed to tough it out. We had our family and friends in our corner, but there was this unspoken understanding that this was our battle to fight, and we didn't want to burden anyone else with it. So we didn't talk about it much. I mean, how do you start a conversation with "Hey, I had a total mental breakdown today—how about you?" Yeah, not the best icebreaker, right?

Our friends, well, they kind of tiptoed away from us during that time. It's like they didn't know how to handle the whole situation and, honestly, neither did we. It was weird, uncharted territory. Everyone seemed to know something was up, but we all just pretended everything was normal. But it wasn't, and that created this sort of awkward tension.

With our families, it was similar. We didn't know whether to act like everything was hunky dory or be honest about what was going on. So we often opted for the "we're fine" route, put on our masks, and then retreated to our respective corners of life. That pretty much summed up our existence for many months.

Katie, she had her own unique battle. The doctors and therapists were working with her, trying to figure out the right mix of meds and counseling to help her through this emotional roller coaster. Balancing self-care with the demands of three little rascals, running a household, and stepping back from her day care gig—it was a juggling act of epic proportions. Despite her Herculean efforts, you could see the exhaustion etched on her face.

We tried to take breaks, go on dates, and even venture on family getaways, but those things require time and money. And we didn't want to impose on our loved ones. We felt this nagging guilt about taking breaks, like we were taking advantage of the support that not everyone had. It was a constant mental struggle, one we wrestled with every single day.

Katie and I were like two peas in a pod, cut from the same cloth. You know how they say opposites attract? Well, that wasn't us. We married someone who mirrored ourselves. We share this deep-seated desire to put others' happiness before our own, a sort of self-imposed martyrdom. We are both peacemakers, the kind of people who'd rather bear their own suffering than see someone else unhappy. Now, pair two peacemakers together, and you've got a bit of a conundrum. It was like a dance of "What do you need?" We'd ask each other, but neither of us wanted to be seen as taking advantage. So we'd both say, "We're fine," hoping the other would insist and take what they wanted. But neither of us budged, stuck in this endless loop of trying to please one another, even if it meant we weren't making ourselves happy.

This dynamic became even more pronounced after the emotional toll our mental health took. We started feeling like burdens to those around us, so we withdrew, not seeking the help we so desperately needed. We pulled away from our relationship, and people probably thought we needed space to heal. But it was quite the opposite. We withdrew because we didn't want to impose on anyone else's already complicated lives. We thought, "Why burden them with our problems when they have their own to deal with?" Our minds played these tricks on us, creating a tangled web of distorted perspectives that hindered our healing.

While Katie was getting the care she deserved, I tried my best too. I talked to counselors and pastors, searching for coping strategies, but it was a tough road. Financially, we took a hit seeing those medical bills pile up. Pay one, and another would arrive, and we'd laughingly joke that we'd be paying off Kobe's hospital bills until he turned eighteen. Well, it didn't quite last that long, but it did take us eight years. Our laughter turned to tears, and eventually, you become so numb to the pain that you just keep going. As blessed as we were, at times, we felt like life was playing a cruel joke on us. You work tirelessly, following what you believe is your God-given calling, only to experience fleeting moments of joy before life throws you a curveball. It was a relentless mental health roller coaster, one that seemed like it would never come to a stop.

So to put it simply, 2019 was a blur. Who can remember that year, especially with what lay ahead? Ah, you know what's about to hit.

As we ventured into 2020, there was a glimmer of hope on the horizon. Katie and I had weathered a turbulent year, and while things hadn't exactly been a walk in the park, they were at least manageable. Then came the big news—baby number four was on the way. Katie was overjoyed; having a big family had always been her dream. However, some people in our circle had questions, especially considering what she had gone through just a year prior. So without getting into specifics, let's just say that not everyone was as thrilled about our announcement as we were. Publicly, they celebrated the baby, but privately, you could almost hear the murmurs: "What are they thinking? Aren't they making their lives unnecessarily complicated?" To be honest, Katie and I had wrestled with those very questions, praying late into the night and battling the same doubts that others had about us. Even in that moment, whether voiced or silent, we felt the weight of judgment from those around us. Nevertheless, we chose to forge ahead.

With baby number four on the way, we knew we needed more space. So we embarked on the daunting task of selling our current house and finding a new one. Yes, I can sense the skepticism now—a baby on the way and the chaos of moving houses. Looking back, we sometimes wonder what we were getting ourselves into. But we had a vision, and we were determined to see it through. We believed we could handle it, and so we dived right in. For the next two months, we poured our efforts into decluttering our home. Our Realtor, as it turned out, had his doubts about our ability to get the house ready in time, too, but we proved him wrong. Then, just three weeks away from putting our house on the market, the world suddenly ground to a halt.

COVID-19 had arrived. For the next few days, we watched as the world came to a standstill. As a family, we adjusted to life indoors with the kids attending school via Zoom, church services going digital, and our only means of connecting with friends and family being through FaceTime. That became our new normal for a while— life on hold. Katie and I exchanged glances and took a deep breath because even as the world outside stopped, we were determined to keep moving forward. After all, we had to find a new place to call home before the baby arrived.

Our house hit the market, and while Katie and I took the kids to the park, potential buyers explored every nook and cranny of our home. It was a seller's dream, with everyone eager to see our house. On the very first day, we received multiple offers, and with that, we embarked on the quest to find our new home. After weeks of tireless searching, we finally stumbled upon our perfect abode. But as all of this unfolded, we were about to face a one-two punch that would make the year even more challenging.

In the midst of 2019, things took a tough turn for my family. My mom dropped a bombshell on us—she had cancer. It was the kind of news that can knock the wind out of you. But we clung to hope, believing that with the right treatment, she'd beat it. Meanwhile, Katie and I were grappling with our own issues. We had to face the fact that 2019 was just a brutal year all around.

My mom, despite her own battle, remained a pillar of strength and faith. She'd tell me that God was looking out for us, and she kept praying for Katie and me. She had this unwavering belief that no matter how tough things got, with Jesus on our side, we'd come out on top. Thinking back to her words now brings a mix of emotions, a kind of bittersweetness. She was our ultimate prayer warrior.

While we were wrestling with our own problems, my mom's health continued to decline. In May of 2020, my mom called a family meeting to discuss her deteriorating condition. It was a heart-wrenching moment when she shared her decision to stop treatment. She wanted to savor the time she had left, enjoying life rather than enduring more medical procedures. So there we were, trying to support her through this, even as we faced our own challenges.

And then came August, the month of my mom's celebration party. We decided to celebrate her life with a big family gathering. It was a beautiful and emotional day, filled with stories, laughter, and tears. I'll never forget the sparkle in my mom's eyes as she watched her family come together, making memories. That was her greatest joy: to see us all united. Her smile from that day still warms my heart. It felt like she had found peace and was ready to meet Jesus.

Amid all the chaos, Katie and I were getting ready to welcome our fourth little one into the world. It might sound a bit crazy with everything else happening—COVID-19, buying and selling a house, my mom's cancer battle—but life sure knows how to throw curveballs, right? And just when we thought we'd seen our fair share of challenges, the doctor hit us with another surprise.

After some extra tests, the doctor told us that our baby had one kidney larger than the other. While it didn't raise immediate alarms, they wanted to keep a close eye on it throughout the pregnancy. I remember sitting there, listening to the doctor's words, feeling strangely unfazed. It's like we'd reached a point where one more piece of bad news couldn't rattle us. I even found myself asking the doctor about the worst-case scenario, and when he mentioned the possibility of a transplant, that numbness turned into a sinking feeling.

Life was a roller coaster, and every day seemed to bring a new challenge. All we could do was hold on to our faith in God and each other. God was our anchor, our safe haven in the storm of pain and uncertainty. We knew we could trust Him to guide us, but we were also leaning on each other for support.

The next few months, life was a whirlwind. We sold our house, moved into a new one, and prepared for the arrival of our fourth bundle of joy. When the big day arrived, we found ourselves back at the hospital, ready for another C-section adventure. Despite it being the year of COVID-19, not much had changed in the delivery room, and Katie seemed more at ease this time.

Koner Ray made his grand entrance into the world at a strapping nine pounds and two ounces. Our hearts swelled with joy as we counted his tiny fingers and toes. We cherished those precious moments together. Later, the doctor shared something astonishing—Koner was a little miracle. During the surgery, she had discovered that the amniotic sac in the womb was incredibly thin and on the verge of bursting. If Koner had stayed in the womb a bit longer, it could have been disastrous for both him and Katie. The doctor said it was like a higher power was looking out for us, ensuring the sac stayed intact. The doctor marveled at how clearly she could see Koner in the sac, hurrying the procedure to avoid any danger. It was a breathtaking moment of grace in the midst of our tumultuous journey.

God was definitely looking out for both Katie and Koner. In the depth of all the unpredictability, we just had to lean on God. Here was a real example of us doing just that. We couldn't control the situation, so we relied on our prayers and trusted that God would guide the doctor. By some miracle, both Mom and baby came out of it strong and healthy, ready to take on whatever came our way. It was funny, though, hearing the doctor's words about 2020 being a year of uncertainty. Like, what else could possibly happen, right?

Koner needed monitoring, but time passed, and then we got the green light to leave the hospital together just a few days after his birth. When we got home, there was this huge sign on our lawn that read, "Congrats, Baby Koner!" The boys were ecstatic to meet their new little brother, and they took turns holding him and smothering him with kisses. We spent hours FaceTiming with friends and family so they could meet the newest member of our crew. For a while there, we felt like life was getting back on track in our new home, and our family was complete and content.

The next month, we made a trip to Chicago to see a specialist who told us that Koner had a blockage in his left kidney. Surgery was a must in order to fix it and hopefully get that kidney working better. We scheduled it for early January, giving us a few months to prepare for the roller coaster ahead. And, boy, were we in for a wild ride.

Jumping ahead in the same month, we paid a visit to my mom, and she got to meet her fifteenth grandchild face to face. Cradling the little one in her arms, her face lit up with pure joy as she marked her seventieth year. The next few weeks whizzed by in a whirlwind, but when we all gathered at my parents' house, it felt like a Thanksgiving unlike any other. Just a few days earlier, Mom's health had taken a downturn, and on Thanksgiving evening, with her family by her side, all of us singing and giving thanks to God for the time we had with Mom, she peacefully passed away. She had achieved two out of the three goals she'd set for herself before her departure. First, she had reached her seventieth birthday, then she'd enjoyed one last Thanksgiving feast with the family, and she was just one week away from her fiftieth wedding anniversary with my dad when she bid her farewell.

The family went through a tough stretch, coming together to remember and honor my mom. It was a challenging time, especially with the whole COVID-19 situation and all the arrangements on our plate. But what really stands out is that my mom got to spend her last days surrounded by family. We shared stories, sang songs, and just stayed by her side. In those moments before she passed, she seemed at peace. No more pain, no more sorrow—she had found comfort in God's embrace.

After the funeral, when we returned home, I remember the silence. It was a stark contrast to the noise and activity of the past days spent with family. In the midst of our chaotic world, I found peace in that quiet.

Once we said goodbye to my family and went back home, we began to prepare for the Christmas season. But not before we got hit with COVID-19 in the family. Yeah, great timing, right? As a family we got through it like we have gotten through many things in our life. This time was no different.

A few weeks passed, and when it came time for Koner's surgery, I looked at his little face and saw a happy, resilient baby ready to face this challenge at such a young age. He bounced back remarkably well. Although we didn't know it then, that would be his only surgery. He does have a mild case of kidney disease, but we're grateful that now we only have to see a specialist once a year. We keep praying for his health and growth, knowing that despite the delays caused by his kidney condition, he's growing into a strong kid who'll tackle any challenges that come his way, inspired by his relentless parents.

As 2021 unfolded, we reflected on how a series of significant events took us by surprise. We experienced the whirlwind of buying and selling a home, the challenges of the COVID-19 pandemic, the joy of welcoming our fourth child into the world, the loss of my mother, and the anxiety of our son's kidney surgery at just five months old. It's been a journey we never could have predicted, and it's a testament to our resilience as a couple and a family.

Resilience isn't just a word to us; it's been the foundation of our entire marriage. We've faced each obstacle head on, never alone, and always with unwavering faith in God. It's the only way we've managed to navigate through these trials with strength and determination—resilience in the face of adversity.

6. Faith in the Unseen

So what's faith, really? I've tossed that word around quite a bit in my writing, but let's break it down. It's all about wholeheartedly trusting in God, handing over the reins and accepting that there are situations where I've got zero control. You see, most of the time, we can shape the outcomes of things in our lives—make them better or worse. But then there are those instances where we're powerless. When I reflect on the roller-coaster ride of the past decade, I see plenty of moments where I had no say in how things unfolded. In those times, I leaned hard on Jesus, believing that He'd not only see us through but also light up the path as we navigated this wild journey called life.

After we had Koner, we kind of decided he'd be the last little one joining our crew. The doctors pretty much confirmed it. I mean, Katie's a champ, and despite everything we've been through, she'd probably be up for having a couple more. But you know what? We feel content with our four amazing kiddos.

Getting used to life with four kids wasn't exactly a cakewalk. We were already pretty wiped out with just three, and we were worried things might get even crazier. We did our best to support each other, sneak in a nap here and there, but our two older boys had outgrown their nap days, and keeping up with their endless energy was a real challenge. These kids had their hands in all sorts of sports, neighborhood stuff, and school events, and life suddenly went from a leisurely stroll to an all-out sprint.

But here's the thing: no matter how crazy life got, it was worth it. Those moments of chaos were balanced by the overwhelming love and joy our family brought us. We laughed together, celebrated victories big and small, and found peace in our faith during challenging times. As parents, we learned the art of multitasking, negotiation, and endless patience.

In those wild and wonderful days, we discovered that family isn't just about blood ties; it's about the bonds we create, the memories we cherish, and the love we share. It's about finding beauty in the messiness of life and embracing every moment, knowing that each day is a gift.

So even when life felt like a whirlwind, we held on to our faith and each other. We knew that no matter what challenges lay ahead, we would face them together, with love as our guiding light.

Then in 2021, as COVID-19 started to loosen its grip, everyone, including us, seemed to kick things into high gear. Our days were packed with travel, parties, events, weddings, vacations—you name it, we did it. Life just went from zero to sixty real quick.

As life kept rolling on, we made some new friends, and I got the chance to baptize quite a few new believers. It felt really good to just go with the flow again. Over the next year, things were looking up. Our kids were learning and growing; Katie and I hit the ten-year mark and were still figuring out this whole partnership and parenting life.

We kind of had it down to a science—counseling when needed, praying as we were seeking God's direction, taking breaks in our busyness, and throwing in celebrations here and there amid the daily hustle. Both Katie and I were genuinely excited about our life's mission, and for a bit there, it felt like we were catching a glimpse of what people call normal in this ever-changing world.

Katie and I finally managed to sneak away for a marriage weekend getaway, which was a rare treat for us. During our time together, we had some deep conversations about the next phase of our marriage journey—building solid relationships and finding mentors to guide us. We were laying the groundwork to keep growing as a couple and as parents, doing all the right things.

But you know, even when you're doing your best, life has a way of throwing curveballs. On Friday, September 2, 2022, I noticed something was off with Katie. She seemed completely drained and unusually quiet and had that distant look in her eyes that I'd seen before. Without hesitation, I arranged for Morna, Katie's mom, to look after our kids and rushed Katie to the hospital.

The uncertainty of the situation weighed heavily on my mind as we made our way to the hospital. Katie's health scare earlier in our marriage still haunted me, and I feared history might be repeating itself. We sat in the waiting room, the minutes ticking by like hours, both of us silently contemplating the unknown.

When the doctors finally examined Katie, the diagnosis was nothing short of shocking. It turned out that she had had a severe anxiety attack that had been getting worse. The medical team went into action, administering treatment and doing everything they could to stop her anxiety from causing further damage.

As I looked at Katie in her hospital bed, hooked up to machines and monitors, my heart swelled with sorrow. Once again, the woman I loved, the mother of our four children, was grappling with yet another mental health crisis. She began experiencing distressing hallucinations and uncontrollable body tremors, eventually slipping into a catatonic state. In this state, she seemed distant and unresponsive, as if she were a world apart. It was a harsh wake-up call, a poignant reminder that life can take an unexpected turn in the blink of an eye, even during seemingly ordinary moments, bringing unforeseen challenges to our doorstep.

Over the next few days, Katie's condition remained critical, and the emotional roller coaster we experienced was unlike anything we had ever faced. We leaned on our faith, praying fervently for her recovery and drawing strength from the support of our family and friends.

It took hours to snap her out of that catatonic state, and let me tell you, it was really tough to see her going through that all over again. But deep down, I knew she wouldn't be coming home anytime soon.

This one hit us out of the blue, and after all these years of life's ups and downs, it had become our new normal. Well, our not-so-normal normal, if you catch my drift. But that's the life we've got, and we're taking it one day at a time.

This is where our faith kicks in, you know? I've come to accept that I'm not the one steering this ship, and our life, well, it's anything but ordinary. But I've got faith in this mysterious, unseen force I call God. He's the creator of life, the one who made everything—the heavens, the earth, all the critters, and even little old me. He has a special plan for me during my time on this planet: worshiping Him and spreading the word that having faith in Jesus means securing a spot in the eternal life beyond, far beyond our time here on earth.

So as long as I'm breathing this earthly air and because God's got so much love for me, I'm trying my best to show some love in return, both to Him and to those sharing this wild ride with me.

All right, I've laid it all out on the table, and believe me, I'm not messing around. If you don't have a relationship with Jesus or you're thinking about recommitting your life to Him again, I'd say it's time you checked out a local church. That's why we are sharing our story. It's not just our sheer determination or our inner strength that's seen Katie and me through all this chaos—it's because we've put our trust in Jesus.

I want you to hear this crystal clear: God loves you, and He's itching for you to get to know Him better so He can help you shake off whatever's been keeping you from finding real peace in your life. I won't sugarcoat it—our life ain't all sunshine and rainbows, as you've clearly gathered. But today, Katie and I have a sense of peace that helps us look past our doubts and uncertainties, all thanks to the hope we've found in Jesus.

Let's go back to that Friday in the hospital with Katie. I remember sitting there, deep in thought about our unpredictable journey, when I got an email notification. It was from my son Kobe, clicking away on his school computer. He asked, "How's Mama doing?"

That email truly hit me different; he was still pretty young and couldn't fully grasp the seriousness of the situation, but his concern shone through those words. I shot back a reply, trying to ease his worries: "She's getting better, and hopefully, we'll be home soon."

Little did I know that "soon" would take a bit longer, and just to add a twist, Katie tested positive for COVID-19. To make things trickier, the hospital had some strict policies, which meant I couldn't stay with her anymore. She had to be quarantined. So there we were, separated once more, this time for a whole week. FaceTime became our lifeline, offering those video calls to catch a glimpse of the kids and each other.

But eventually, after what felt like forever, Katie got the green light to come home. She started her outpatient treatment, and I have to say, I was seriously impressed with how far she'd come. It was a world away from our previous experiences, where she'd been heavily medicated and lost in a fog of uncertainty. This time around, she was more aware of her recovery, less reliant on meds, and slowly but surely, emerging from the haze that had clouded her before.

I mean, Katie could really explain how she felt in that state better, but let me tell you, she felt like she had a better grip on things this time. She could handle whatever came her way with more confidence compared to the past. And you know what? It's thanks to those amazing doctors, counselors, nurses, and therapists who've been there every step of the way, helping her through this mental health journey. They've been like our guiding stars, and we owe them a big thanks for getting her to this point.

It all started with our rock-solid faith in God, the kind of faith that kept us going through thick and thin, even when life threw us curveballs. Our faith has been like a sturdy anchor, helping us weather the storms, not just for ourselves but for our family's sake and our own well-being. Christ is the cornerstone of our lives, and Jesus is our Rock.

7. Next to Normal

For months, I was on a quest to figure out how to put into words what Katie and I had been going through. Expressing the pain and struggles was tough, even with friends. Mental health had taken a real toll on my family, but how do you explain that?

I'd been mulling this over for weeks when a surprise came our way. You see, Katie and I are subscribers to our local theater. We pay a yearly fee and get to watch some pretty amazing shows. In 2023, we decided to check out a play called *Next to Normal*. Honestly, I hadn't heard of it, and I didn't bother looking up what it was about. I got an email warning us about adult content and mental health themes, but I brushed it off because we watch so many shows in a year.

So there we were, getting ready for our date night. We had a couple of drinks, took our seats in the theater, and let the show begin. As soon as that opening number hit the stage and set the tone, Katie and I exchanged a glance, and it hit us both like a ton of bricks. Without saying a word, we knew this show was about to spill the beans on the mental struggles we'd been grappling with for the past six years.

Our eyes got all misty as we listened to the husband and wife in the play pouring their hearts out, and Katie and I held hands, ready to see fragments of our own story unfold right before us.

Now, if you haven't caught this show yet, seriously, take a quick detour to Google and get the lowdown. I promise you, I won't be able to capture its awesomeness with words alone. And if the chance ever comes your way to see it live, believe me, it's well worth your time and money. Katie and I are huge fans of Broadway theater, even though they often tackle some heavy topics. But they've got this knack for telling stories that hit home, especially for those of us dealing with mental health stuff. There's just something about the magic of live theater that adds a whole new layer to the experience.

Let me try my best to lay it out for you: as the performance continued, we were drawn deeper into the lives of the characters onstage. The husband's desperation to save his wife from the grips of mental illness mirrored my own feelings of helplessness during our darkest moments. The wife's struggle to hold on to her identity and the pain it caused her family resonated with Katie's experiences.

Through the powerful music and raw emotion on display, we felt an unspoken connection with the characters. It was as if the playwright had captured the essence of our own journey and translated it into a universal story of love, loss, and resilience.

As we watched the characters navigate therapy sessions, medication changes, and the daily challenges of living with mental illness, we saw our own reflections in their struggles. The isolation, the fear, and the uncertainty felt all too familiar.

Throughout the play, Katie and I exchanged knowing glances and held each other's hands a little tighter. It was as if *Next to Normal* had given us a safe space to acknowledge the pain and challenges we had faced as a couple. It was a reminder that we were not alone in our journey and that our experiences were shared by others.

Now don't get me wrong, this story is not an exact match, but I mention it because the play revolved around a specific incident that kicked off the main character's mental health journey.

As we watched the show, Katie and I stumbled upon moments that kind of helped us feel each other's pain a bit better. It's funny how it happened, really, like a light bulb suddenly flicking on.

See, when it came to me, I was all about fixing stuff. If Katie told me everything was cool, I'd take her word for it and dive into handling our other life stuff, you know, like taking care of the kids or sorting out bills. Now Katie, she had this endless stream of thoughts racing through her head. She loaded up her plate with so much stuff that, honestly, it was a miracle her body kept up. But she didn't stop 'cause in her eyes, a mom, a wife, had to power through and get all those things on her never-ending to-do list done.

Watching that play made us realize that we had our own unique ways of dealing with the chaos in our lives. It was like a mirror reflecting our struggles and strengths. I had a newfound appreciation for the sheer resilience and determination Katie exhibited daily. On the flip side, Katie saw how my instinct to fix things sometimes overshadowed the importance of just being there for her, listening without trying to find solutions.

After the show, we walked back to our car in silence, deep in thought. It was as if the characters onstage had given us a glimpse into our own hearts and minds. We were eager to talk about what we'd just witnessed, how it resonated with our own experiences, and how we could better support each other in this journey through mental health challenges. It marked a turning point for us, a moment of enlightenment that would shape the way we faced our battles together.

As we wondered how we'd ended up in this crazy cycle, we knew that we had lost sight of who we were in God's eyes, slipping into the roles of husband and wife, Mom and Dad. Life kept getting busier, and we started thinking it was all normal. Truth is, we were just slapping a Band-Aid on the mess we were feeling with all sorts of distractions that didn't really help. We prayed, we read the Bible, we had our faith, sure, but deep down, we were avoiding the real issues. And me? Well, I pretty much threw in the towel. I got lost in the drama of movies, escaping my reality and pretending like everything was just fine.

As we reflected on that fateful night at the theater, we were grateful for the unexpected gift *Next to Normal* gave us. It made us realize that we were never really OK but we kept telling ourselves we were. That's something a lot of us do, right? Pretend that our lives are hunky dory, that we've got it better than most. So we push on, do more, chase after more, thinking that eventually, everything will magically fall into place. That was me, for years on end, until we got hit with our first reality check.

We went through the motions, living as if everything was picture perfect when, in truth, it was just next to normal. It took a powerful theatrical experience to jolt us awake and make us realize that our lives, our struggles, and our journey toward healing were not only valid but also worth sharing with the world. We found the courage to confront our own next-to-normal existence and turn it into a source of inspiration for others walking a similar path.

8. A Better Tomorrow

Every day, I'm just hoping the next one's a bit better than the last. You know how life can be: full of surprises. But hope keeps me looking ahead to a brighter tomorrow. Still, I don't forget the work that needs doing today because it's what sets the stage for tomorrow. Life's like that sometimes—you do everything by the book, and things can still go sideways. There's that old saying, right? Tomorrow isn't promised, so I've learned to appreciate the people and things in my life today.

The other day, I was picking up my little three-year-old, Koner, from school, and it hit me how much joy he finds in the little things. As we hopped into the car, he was practically bubbling over with excitement, pointing at everything in sight. Cars driving past, the big yellow school bus, even a loud motorcycle zooming by—he was living in the moment. It got me thinking, considering how close we came to losing him. But here he is, filling our lives with joy. It reminded me to find joy in life's simple pleasures and appreciate every day.

To all our awesome friends who've been there with us on this crazy ride, whether we came running or tried to hide, we just want to say a big thank-you. Whether our time together was a quick chat or years of hanging out, we cherish every moment. Your love and support mean the world to us. You had our backs when we needed it most, and now we've got yours in our prayers. You all played a huge part in helping us through, and we can't thank you enough for that. Life is full of unexpected twists and turns, but with friends like you by our side, we know we can weather any storm that comes our way.

To our dear families, you've been there for us in the tough times, popping in with food and bringing smiles to our faces. You've cared for our boys like they were your own, and we can't thank you enough. Your support, even when we needed some space, meant a lot. And when we called for help, you didn't hesitate. We appreciate you more than words can express.

To our moms, you've prayed with us, shed tears alongside us, and given your all for us. Claudia and Morna, your dedication to your children's well-being has been unwavering. Your support means the world to us, and it's because of your love and guidance that our kids will grow up understanding the true value of family. Your stories of love and kindness will echo through generations. Your unwavering faith in God has been a guiding light through all the challenges life has thrown your way. It's this faith that connects us, that has driven you to work tirelessly to assist us in our journey. Your ultimate goal is to show our children God's love through your actions. Thank you, Mom. Your love and dedication have made all the difference.

To our boys, you're a big part of our family, and we just want to say thanks for being here with us on this wild ride. When you're older and reading this book, you might be like "Whoa, Mom and Dad's life was something else!" Our wish for each of you is to live a life full of purpose, following the path God has in store for you. So keep seeking God's guidance and aim to make a positive difference in Jesus's name. One day, we'll all meet Him, and that's when the real celebration begins. Your journey in faith and love will carry on the legacy of our family for generations to come.

To my amazing wife, Katie, I want to give you a big shout-out for letting me tell our story. Remember when I first pitched the idea of sharing our wild ride with the world? You were like "Whoa, slow down. I'm not sure I'm ready for that." And honestly, I was right there with you, hesitating and finding excuses to procrastinate. Life got crazy, right?

But then, in the midst of all the chaos, God gave me a wake-up call. He said, "Start writing." So here we are.

Katie, you're a rock star. Even when you doubt your own strength, let me remind you that you're a force to be reckoned with. I've seen you read parts of this book, sometimes with tears, and it's like watching a superhero in action.

We've been through a lot, and while I hope this book wraps up our crazy adventures, if it doesn't, I'm not worried. It's our faith in God and the promises we've made to each other that keep us going. We're in this for the long haul, my love. I grow deeper in love with you each and every day.

Your unwavering support, your ability to keep our family together through thick and thin, and your boundless love inspire me. You've been the anchor in the storms, the light in the darkest nights, and the reason I smile every morning. Our love story is a testament to the beauty of commitment and the strength of love. I cherish every moment we've shared and look forward to the countless adventures that lie ahead, knowing that with you by my side, there's nothing we can't conquer. Thank you for being the incredible woman you are.

Every day is like hitting the reset button, right? A fresh start, a brand-new sunrise, and a chance to give life another go. It's kinda funny how the sun just keeps on doing its thing, making its rounds, while we're down here trying to make sense of it all. It's a bit like being the new kid in town, isn't it? We might be rookies in this big ol' universe, but you know what? God's been here for a while, He's seen it all, and that's oddly comforting. So even though I'll admit I get a little jittery and have my fair share of doubts, I'm not throwing in the towel on tomorrow. Nope, I'm here for the long haul, ready to see what's in store. Until my time's up, I'm holding on to hope that tomorrow's gonna be a good one. And you better believe I won't forget how we've powered through all those yesterdays.

As we're wrapping up this part of our journey, I just wanted to say thanks for being a part of it. Life's an adventure, and we've all got our own stories to tell. This is just a chapter in ours. Remember, you're never alone in whatever you're going through. We're all in this together, writing our stories as we go. So take care, and may God's blessings shine on you.

In these moments of reflection, I'm feeling thankful for the simple joys and big lessons life's thrown our way. From the tiniest victories to the toughest trials, they've all shaped us into who we are today. Our shared journey has been a testament to resilience, faith, and the enduring power of love.

Let's not forget all those sunrises we've watched together, each one representing a fresh chance to embrace life's mysteries. Even though we don't have all the answers, we'll keep exploring, learning, and growing, always hanging on to the hope of a brighter tomorrow.

So here's to new beginnings, cherished memories, the unwavering support of loved ones, and the faith that guides our steps. May your own life story be filled with love, laughter, and adventure, and may you find inspiration in the promise of each new day. Until we meet again in another story, take care.

About the Author

Israel Ruiz resides in the suburban landscapes of Chicagoland alongside his wife, a loving partnership of 12 years that has been blessed with the laughter and energy of four boys. As a devoted pastor, Israel's passion lies in helping individuals discover who God is and guiding them toward finding true freedom in their lives. His journey, intertwined with that of his family, has been a lifelong odyssey filled with both challenges and triumphs.

Born and raised in Holland, Michigan, Israel grew up in a home where his parents, driven by love for God, endeavored to provide the best for their children. With one brother and three sisters, family has always been a cornerstone of his life, and the closeness they share remains a source of strength and support. Recognizing the profound importance of extended family, Israel acknowledges that their collective perseverance through life's trials would not have been possible without their unwavering presence.

Initially drawn to the field of Engineering, Israel's path took a significant turn as he discovered a deeper calling in the realm of church ministry. Pursuing this newfound passion, he embarked on a transformative journey at Moody Bible Institute. It was here that he not only deepened his understanding of his faith but also honed his ability to be a resilient and grounded guide for those who crossed his path.

Israel considers himself blessed to be precisely where God has intended him to be. As he anticipates the future, he is eager to embrace the adventures and opportunities that God has in store. Through his writing and ministry, Israel seeks to share the wisdom gained from his experiences, providing insights that blend faith with the realities of life, and offering a helping hand to those seeking solace and purpose.

Get ready to embark on a journey of inspiration and self-discovery with Israel Ruiz, a pastor, family man, and guide who believes that life's struggles are best faced together, with faith and a strong foundation in reality.

Made in United States
Troutdale, OR
01/13/2024